#LiveIntentionally
52-Week Challenge

by
Mark D. Bush

In loving memory of my
Mother, Chandlyn Anthony

Table of Contents

Forward

By Elizabeth Higgins

On paper, 2015 was a great year in my life. I had an awesome job that I loved, with great people to work with. The job also gave me financial stability, something I hadn't had since I got out of the Air Force in 2007. My relationship status had never been better, my boyfriend is an amazing man doing amazing things. We had a healthy two year old daughter together and my 11 year old daughter from a previous marriage was doing great. Our home life was "perfect". Everything was perfect actually. Yet this year was remarkably harder than normal. I was in a deep depression and didn't know why. In the past, I had been diagnosed with PTSD from my time in combat during Operation Iraqi Freedom, but I worked really hard for years to be "normal" and hadn't had serious symptoms in years. I went back to therapy and got back on medication. Yet nothing was working. I couldn't be happy, even though I knew I should be, life was good...great actually.

My good friend, Mark, was always good about checking in on me from time to time. We were stationed together at the Air Force Academy, Colorado. We also served in Iraq 2004-2005, we have a bond that will never end. One day, he talked to me about some things he was dealing, I was floored. Here I was having a hard time getting out of bed with a "perfect" life and he had real issues going on and he didn't let it get him down. During our conversation, Mark shared his coping mechanisms with me. He shared his "Reflection Sunday", a list of things going on with his friends and family. Every Sunday he picks one thing to do for someone he loves, where it be calling a friend or buying a shirt someone mentioned they wanted and sending it to them to let them know, someone was paying attention to them. He did something for people in his life so they knew someone was thinking about them. The best part of it was what it did for him. It brought him from being down about his life to feeling full, satisfied, and gave him PURPOSE. It was exactly what I was looking missing. From then on every time I'm having a hard day or feeling down I do something for someone else. I send a gift card to a friend far away or something as small as giving a "shout out" on social media for accomplishments someone achieved. Sometimes I buy a coffee for a stranger, pay for parking, give an unusually large tip for a car wash. It literally brightens the day for others, but in return I feel a bigger purpose in my own life. It makes my heart full and I can stay positive knowing I may have given a smile to someone in need. I'm told I could struggle for the rest of my life with depression, but now I have a tool that works to fight those negative feelings thanks to Mark sharing his ideas of living intentionally.

Preface

"Remember whose name you have," my pops, Corby Bush Sr., would tell us before leaving the house, growing up. I knew exactly what he meant; I represent my family in everything I do, good or bad. Here's the thing, my last name was not always Bush, I was born Mark Anthony. When I think about proud moments, I can't help but think about how proud I was to become a Bush.

I was born to the beautiful Chicagoan, Chandlyn Anthony and her husband Randy Anthony. I came into this world with my twin brother, affectionately known as my "wombmate", Marlon Anthony, November 22, 1982. My parents separated after my mother filed a battery complaint against Randy, after a series of arguments had turned into violent fights. On March 23, 1986, two weeks after my parents had separated; Marlon and I were in the kitchen with our mother as she washed dishes. On that Sunday morning, we heard the crashing sound of our front door slamming against the wall as it was furiously opened. It was Randy. He came into the house arguing with our mother. The arguing turned into a violent fight and progressed to Randy beating our mother with a telephone receiver. The struggle my mother endured ended when Randy stabbed her four times in her abdomen. My mother fell to the kitchen floor where a pool of blood surrounded her lifeless body. My brother and I were three-years-old and understood everything that had happened, our mother was gone.

Randy left our house and drove to the train station on Pulaski Road and Lake Street. He stood on the edge of the train platform where he removed his wallet and set it down next to him. As onlookers watched, Randy warned them to stay back. He yelled, "Tell my mother I'm sorry," before jumping in front of an arriving train. On that day, my life was forever changed.

Without hesitation, my then uncle, Corby Bush adopted my twin brother and me, as well as our eldest brother, Jason, who is three years older than we are.

Corby Bush, 24-years-old, was married to Yvonne

Bush of Maywood, IL and father of Kristen Bush, who was one year old at the time. Being 33 years old, right now, I couldn't have imagined the enormous amount of responsibility that had been thrust upon him.

For the longest time, I referred to my mother's brother as Uncle Corby. Even though he was my adoptive father, I was still his nephew. I never felt unloved or unequally loved as his child. However, I felt embarrassed when people would ask about my last name. Why wasn't it the same? I remember the way members of or church made us feel. They made us feel like we were inferior to our cousins. They didn't treat us the same. I felt people made a fuss over and loved them more and we were the extra baggage.

When I was younger, I felt ashamed that I didn't have a mom or dad of my own. As the years passed, that feeling changed drastically. The dynamic of our family changed, as well. We were no longer nephews and cousins; we were sons, brothers and sisters. My uncle wouldn't respond unless we called him, "father". We had to consciously be trained to call my uncle "father". I remember people used to mock us because we called him father. It sounded too proper for some. I was proud to call him father. He was just that.

It was twelve days before our seventeenth birthday; my father was keeping a surprise from us. He was changing our last name to Bush, my mother's maiden name, but more importantly, his name. Changing our last name wasn't the surprise; he was giving us a middle name and wouldn't tell us until our court date. Giving us our middle names was his way of being able to name *his* sons. The anticipation was killing me, I had always wanted a middle name, and I had no idea what it would be. On that day, I went from Mark Anthony to Mark Devin Bush. You know how some people hate their middle name or don't want people to know what it is? I was incredibly proud of mine. I think I would have been proud if my middle name was Deerwood. It wasn't about the name. It was about the man who gave it to me. I was now a Bush, and like my father used to tell us, "Remember who you represent." I represented the Bush family name.

It wasn't until I started writing this book, that I ever asked my father why he named me Devin. He told me that Devin meant, "Victorious leader and strong will". He went on to say, "it means harmony or poet, like a person who knows how to bring things together. That's why it came to mean victorious leader and strong will."

I can remember the countless conversations my father and I had when I was a child. I would sit on the closed toilet lid in his bathroom and listen to him talk while he shaved. My father shaved with a kitchen butter knife. Having sensitive skin, he would use shaving powder that he would mix in a coffee cup. While talking, he would make eye contact with me after every stroke of his butter knife against his thick beard. He would ask, "Mark, you understand what I'm saying?" My father would talk to me about the only things a man has, his name and his integrity. One day when I was about eleven or twelve, my father was talking to me. As I sit here and write, I can vividly remember how proud I was of who my father was. At that point in my life, my father was 31, raising eight children (my two brothers and me, four children of his own, and his other two nephews), founded his first church in Oak Park, IL, all while attending Moody Bible Institute for his undergraduate degree. My father was definitely someone to admire. I looked up at him and told him, "Father, I want to be just like you when I grow up." I have never forgotten his words, something that drives me today, "Son, I want you to be better than me." There have been many times in my life that I honestly do not have any idea of how that would even been possible. My father is a world-renowned, well sought-after, Pentecostal Bishop with the Church of God In Christ, Inc. Here's the thing, we will never know if we don't try.

When I was younger, I silently struggled with the loss of my mother. There was a point I didn't understand why I had to lose MY mother. I didn't have a chance to have memories of her scent, her voice, her touch, or what she looked like, without a picture. I felt robbed. My father was preaching one Sunday. He said something that changed my life, "Everything happens for a reason, God has a purpose for everything He does." It changed my outlook on my situation: I was not a victim, I was a victor.

I never knew what kept Randy from taking the lives of my brother and me. We were in the same room. I was not a victim. God spared my life because I had a purpose to fulfill. My purpose was to live intentionally. To live with a sense of purpose. Intentionally impact everything I do and every person I come across. I occasionally receive messages asking how I keep a positive, upbeat, outlook on life. I want to put my thought process and outlook on paper. I want to share, to inspire and uplift as many people as possible. Isn't that what life's about? Impact...Impacting the people around us and everything we touch. It has to be a conscious and intentional decision. Change your mindset...you'll change your life...you'll impact lives.

In my initial brainstorming phase of *#LiveIntentionally*, I started compiling stories of the impact my life has had on others by living intentionally. While writing, I felt a reader could be taken back by the style of my writing. It could possibly be viewed as a pretentious, "look at me" story. I stopped writing and began thinking of how I could get my point across to any reader; those who know me and those who do not.

The idea hit me while driving through downtown Atlanta. I would create an experience for the reader. If my intentions were to impact a reader's life, the reader needs to *feel* an intentional life, not just read about it.

Introduction

The idea of this challenge came to me after several conversations with a childhood friend of mine, Marcia Collins. Marcia and I talk often about the things we're up to and have kept in touch for a little over 18 years. Marcia, along with a few other friends of mine who have followed me on social media, often see my many posts and pictures of what I'm up to and what I'm working on. They usually send me text messages asking what it is that I do that keeps me motivated and positive. I simply reply, "I focus on others." Which is usually followed by the question, "How?"

I usually share with them how I intentionally take my focus off of me and what may be bothering me. This is not to be confused with ignoring my problems. I don't sulk, or as my mother would say, "have a pity party," for myself. I usually do two things to cope with negativity and depression. First, I draw attention away from myself and reflect on the

1

things my family, friends, or co-workers may be dealing with. Then, I intentionally "make someone's day". Nothing crazy, I do intentional acts of kindness- random act for the individual receiving the kindness, but very much calculated on my end. This LIFE CHANGING journal invites you to love intentionally, through my Reflection Sundays and "Intentional Acts of Kindness"…not random acts of kindness, there is nothing random about it.

REFLECTION SUNDAYS

Reflection Sundays is something I came up with a while ago. I found myself at what I thought, at the time, was the hardest time of my life. I kept falling into a deep depression; I refused to see the light at the end of the tunnel. Like most, I struggled alone…I didn't want to appear "weak".

I could hear my mom in the back of my head saying, "there's no time for pity parties". I remember I picked up a pen and note pad and began writing:

> *Joey Oberndorfer –Police Academy grad Oct 15*
> *Faris Flournoy – Primecare Home Care growth*
> *Nathan Hawkins – Assignment and SOS*
> *Father – Healthy Recovery*
> *Riley Gill – Body Building Competition May 23*

Josh O. – Birth of his son Elijah Jeremiah due Aug
Aaron Marquez – Dog Lobo surgery May 27
Jamie Romo – Nursing School
Brian Creswell – Lost mother June 3

Every Sunday, I would come to this list to pray for, think about, and communicate with the individuals on the list. I would send a text or call the people on my list to encourage, check up, and listen to the person on the other end of my phone. It was all about them. I was just there for them.

THE CHALLENGE

Over the course of the next 52-weeks, I challenge you to take my weekly "Intentional Acts of Kindness" and brighten someone's day. The challenges will give you ideas for things to do for your family, friends, co-workers, employees, employers, or neighbors. However, there's a twist. Some challenges will force you to step out of your comfort zone. If you accept my challenge, you will also be tasked with doing things for your least favorite person at work and that family member you don't talk to anymore.

Once your challenge is complete, you can "log" your experience, and intentionally use the "hashtag" provided in your social media post the day you complete your challenge. Every fourth week will consist of the same challenge, "Intentionally Meet New People". You will be challenged to talk to a person you've never talked to before or someone you may know nothing about. Use this challenge to find out their "story" and how you can be a friend to them.

Lastly, you will be responsible for creating and maintaining your "Reflection Sunday" list every week. The concept of this challenge is to intentionally change your behavior. When we change our behavior, we change the world!

Join our *closed* Facebook community to share your experiences during this challenge:
www.facebook.com/groups/LiveIntentionally

Follow me:
Twitter: @MrBeIntentional
Periscope: @MrBeIntentional
Facebook : www.facebook.com/MrBeIntentional

#*Reflection Sunday*

1. Faris Flournoy — Primecare Home Care

2.

3.

Join our closed Facebook community to share your experiences during this challenge:
www.facebook.com/groups/LiveIntentionally

5

#*Reflection Sunday*

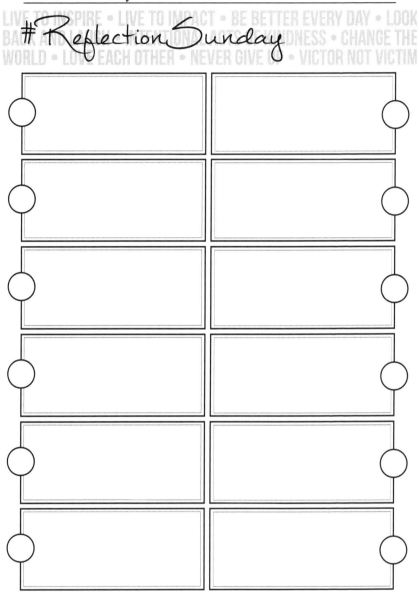

Join our closed Facebook community to share your experiences during this challenge:
www.facebook.com/groups/LiveIntentionally

6

#ReflectionSunday

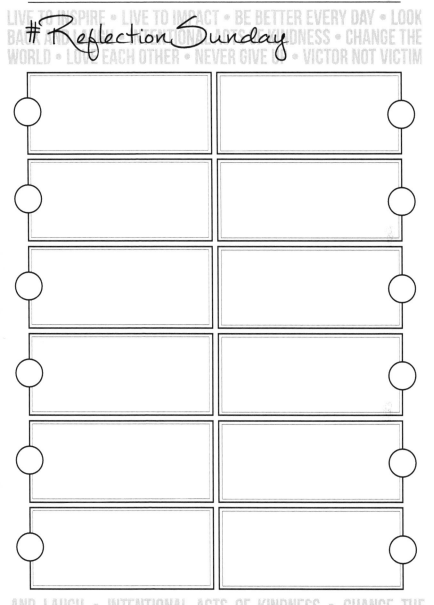

Join our closed Facebook community to share your experiences during this challenge:
www.facebook.com/groups/LiveIntentionally

7

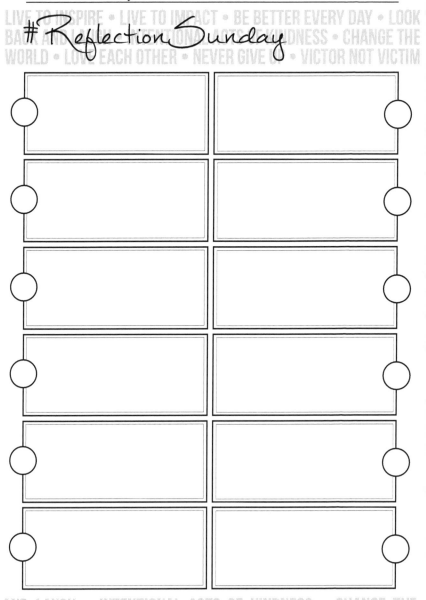

#ReflectionSunday

Join our closed Facebook community to share your experiences during this challenge:
www.facebook.com/groups/LiveIntentionally

8

#ReflectionSunday

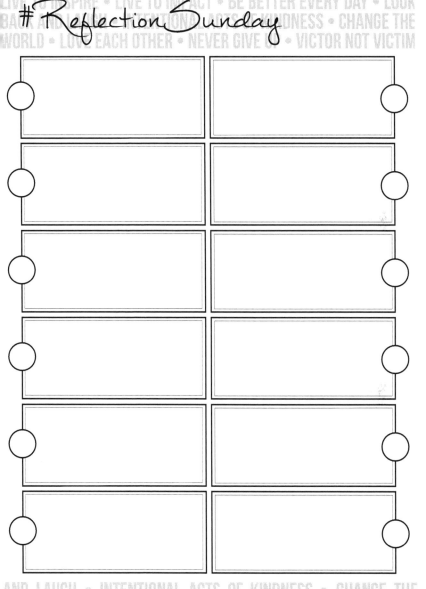

Join our closed Facebook community to share your experiences during this challenge:
www.facebook.com/groups/LiveIntentionally

#Reflection Sunday

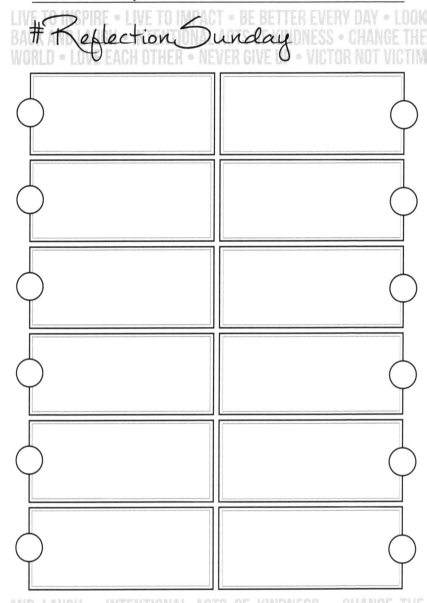

Join our closed Facebook community to share your experiences during this challenge:
www.facebook.com/groups/LiveIntentionally

10

#Reflection Sunday

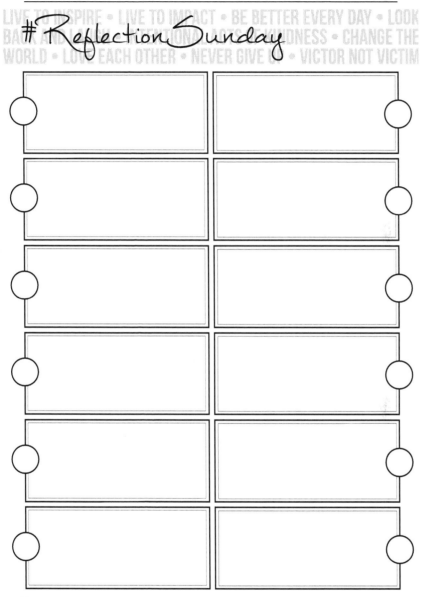

Join our closed Facebook community to share your experiences during this challenge:
www.facebook.com/groups/LiveIntentionally

11

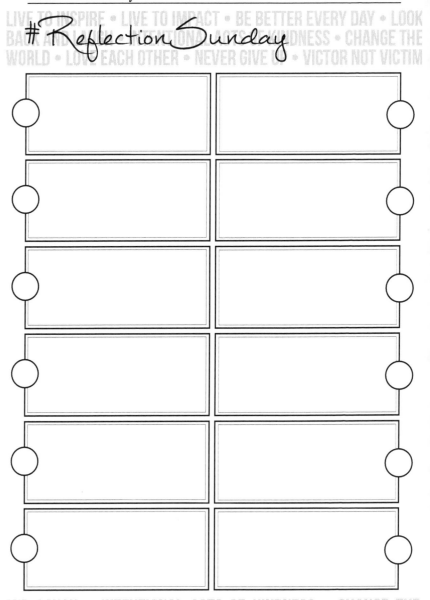

#ReflectionSunday

Join our closed Facebook community to share your experiences during this challenge:
www.facebook.com/groups/LiveIntentionally

12

#ReflectionSunday

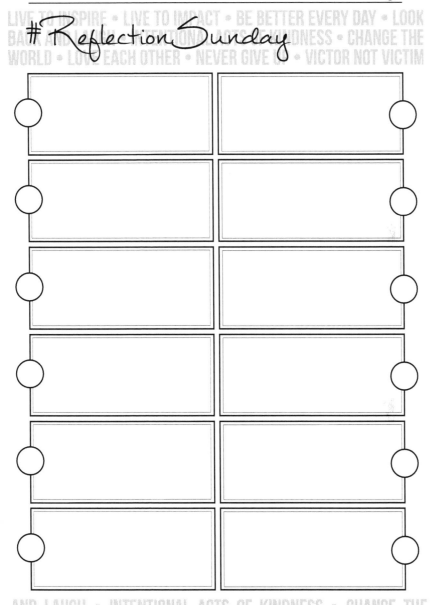

Week 1

At the end of your workday, intentionally write a short message to two of your co-workers or employees letting them know how much you appreciate them. Leave the message at their work center to be surprised by their next shift.

#IntentionallyAppreciate

Recipient of your Challenge:

Recipient's Reaction:

How did it make you feel?

Week 2

Intentionally invite a friend you haven't seen or talked to for a while to grab coffee to catch up. If that friend is unavailable, keep going down the list until you find one who has time.

#IntentionallyCatchUp

Recipient of your Challenge:

Recipient's Reaction:

How did it make you feel?

<u>Week 3</u>

Intentionally buy or make Brownies or some back goods for the office, neighbors, or stranger

#IntentionallyBakeGoods

Recipient of your Challenge:

Recipient's Reaction:

How did it make you feel?

<u>Week 4</u>

Intentionally strike up a conversation with a complete stranger. Learn two things about them and don't forget to log your experience

#IntentionallyMeetNewPeople

Recipient of your Challenge:

Recipient's Reaction:

How did it make you feel?

Week 5

Intentionally write a letter addressed to "My Mail Carrier" and place it in your neighborhood post box, in your mailbox with the flag up, or take it to your local post office. Don't forget to include your address so they know where it came from.

#IntentionallyYouGotMail

Recipient of your Challenge:

Recipient's Reaction:

How did it make you feel?

Week 6

Pick a few friends and intentionally handwrite a letter to each of them explaining what they mean to you. Place them in the mail and let it be a surprise to them. Believe me, they'll let you know when they've received it.

#IntentionallyWrite

Recipient of your Challenge:

Recipient's Reaction:

How did it make you feel?

Week 7

We all know someone of the same gender who's single. Take some time and intentionally invite that person or more to dinner.

#IntentionallyHangingOut

Recipient of your Challenge:

Recipient's Reaction:

How did it make you feel?

<u>Week 8</u>

Intentionally strike up a conversation with a complete stranger. Learn two things about them and don't forget to log your experience

#IntentionallyMeetNewPeople

Recipient of your Challenge:

Recipient's Reaction:

How did it make you feel?

Week 9

Use this week to intentionally pack up old items of clothes, toys, etc. Donate them to a family who could use them or donate them to a thrift store in your community.

#IntentionallyDonate

Recipient of your Challenge:

Recipient's Reaction:

How did it make you feel?

Week 10

Intentionally assist your least favorite person with a task and take the time to get to know them a little better.

#IntentionallyWorkingOnIt

Recipient of your Challenge:

Recipient's Reaction:

How did it make you feel?

Week 11

Intentionally call a Family member you haven't talked to in years due to personal or family disputes. Humbly attempt to work things out. If nothing more, check and see how they're doing.

#IntentionallyForgive

Recipient of your Challenge:

Recipient's Reaction:

How did it make you feel?

Week 12

Intentionally send your primary care physician a card or letter of appreciation. If you're feeling generous, include a gift card for two to a restaurant.

#IntentionallyThankADoc

Recipient of your Challenge:

Recipient's Reaction:

How did it make you feel?

<u>Week 13</u>

Intentionally strike up a conversation with a complete stranger. Learn two things about them and don't forget to log your experience

#IntentionallyMeetNewPeople

Recipient of your Challenge:

Recipient's Reaction:

How did it make you feel?

Week 14

Intentionally offer and insist on mowing your neighbor's lawn, take them something fresh out of the oven, or something specially made for them...the neighbor you don't like. Come on, it's a challenge...did you think I'd make it that easy?!

#IntentionallyLoveThyNeighbor

Recipient of your Challenge:

Recipient's Reaction:

How did it make you feel?

Week 15

Intentionally send each of your siblings a gift card to a restaurant along with a card or letter letting them know how much they mean to you. If you don't have a sibling, choose three of your closest friends. Invite them to dinner at that restaurant if you want, you've already paid!

#IntentionallyLoveMySiblings

Recipient of your Challenge:

Recipient's Reaction:

How did it make you feel?

<u>Week 16</u>

This is an EASY challenge: Intentionally give a "high-five" to every stranger you see, strike up a conversation, share with them your experience with this challenge you're doing and the impact it's had on your life so far.

#IntentionallyPassItOn

Recipient of your Challenge:

Recipient's Reaction:

How did it make you feel?

Week 17

Intentionally strike up a conversation with a complete stranger. Learn two things about them and don't forget to log your experience

#IntentionallyMeetNewPeople

Recipient of your Challenge:

Recipient's Reaction:

How did it make you feel?

Week 18

In honor of National Nurse Day, Intentionally send your favorite nurse a card...this could be a family member, friend, or hospital nurse. Complete a "Customer Satisfaction Survey" on your next visit to the hospital, and give her a raving review. Let's show them some love!

#IntentionallyLoveMyNurse

Recipient of your Challenge:

Recipient's Reaction:

How did it make you feel?

Week 19

Intentionally buy a few $5-7 gift cards from your favorite coffee shop and give them to any Police Officer you come across. Even if it means stopping by the police station...let's thank them for their service.

#IntentionallySupportThePolice

Recipient of your Challenge:

Recipient's Reaction:

How did it make you feel?

Week 20

Each Day this week, find a different motivational quote and share it with someone you think needs it. Starting on Monday, go one full day without complaining. Intentionally stop yourself if you're about to complain. If you complain, your challenge starts over the next day. Keep a tally of how many times you complained or stopped yourself from complaining and log it in your journaling for this challenge.

#IntentionallyStayPositive

Recipient of your Challenge:

Recipient's Reaction:

How did it make you feel?

Week 21

Intentionally send a military friend some sort of care package. This could be anything from a letter, package of snacks, magazines, etc. Something to let them know you're thinking of them and you appreciate their sacrifice. If you don't know anyone, see if a friend has someone you could do something for.

#IntentionallySupportTheTroops

Recipient of your Challenge:

Recipient's Reaction:

How did it make you feel?

Week 22

Intentionally strike up a conversation with two complete strangers. Learn four things about them and don't forget to log your experience.

#IntentionallyMeetNewPeople

Recipient of your Challenge:

Recipient's Reaction:

How did it make you feel?

Week 23

Make a list about the things you like about your *least* favorite person at work. Intentionally take some time in your day and in your own way, share those things with that person.

#IntentionallyGetOverIt

Recipient of your Challenge:

Recipient's Reaction:

How did it make you feel?

Week 24

Intentionally tip your Barber/Beautician/Hair Stylist double or triple the amount you usually tip.

#IntentionallyTip

Recipient of your Challenge:

Recipient's Reaction:

How did it make you feel?

Week 25

Choose a co-worker or employee, and intentionally mow their lawn. If you're not good at mowing lawn, pay a neighborhood kid to take on the chore.

#IntentionallyFreshCutGrass

Recipient of your Challenge:

Recipient's Reaction:

How did it make you feel?

Week 26

Intentionally strike up a conversation with two complete strangers. Learn four things about them and don't forget to log your experience.

#IntentionallyMeetNewPeople

Recipient of your Challenge:

Recipient's Reaction:

How did it make you feel?

<u>Week 27</u>

CONGRATULATIONS!!!

You are half way through the year and if you started in January, you're half way through your challenge. Use this week to reflect on the impact your life has had on others through INTENTIOANLLY seeking people out to brighten their day. Your intentional acts of kindness have gone a long way. Consider buying a few copies of *#LiveIntentionally: 52-Week Challenge* and passing your challenge on to others. Use the next page to log your experience.

#IntentionallyReflect

Join our *closed* Facebook community to tell us about your experience:
www.facebook.com/groups/LiveIntentionally

Twitter: @MrBeIntentional
Periscope: @MrBeIntentional
Facebook : www.facebook.com/MrBeIntentional

Recipient of your Challenge:

Recipient's Reaction:

How did it make you feel?

Week 28

The summer will be coming to an end soon and children will be back in school. Intentionally pick up a few school supplies for a family you think could use the help.

BONUS: Find 2 or 3 families you could assist.

#IntentionallySupply

Recipient of your Challenge:

Recipient's Reaction:

How did it make you feel?

Week 29

Intentionally call two cousins you haven't talked to in a while. Take some time this week to catch up with both of them.

BONUS: Meet up for lunch or dinner and do it in person.

#IntentionallyCatchUp

Recipient of your Challenge:

Recipient's Reaction:

How did it make you feel?

Week 30

Intentionally strike up a conversation with two complete strangers. Learn four things about them and don't forget to log your experience.

BONUS: If you go out to eat, grab coffee, or receive any type of service this week, intentionally ask to speak to the manager and give a compliment about the person who served you.

#IntentionallyMeetNewPeople

Recipient of your Challenge:

Recipient's Reaction:

How did it make you feel?

<u>Week 31</u>

Intentionally make someone dinner.

BONUS: Make dinner and intentionally make enough to take to a few homeless people in your community.

#IntentionallyCook

Recipient of your Challenge:

Recipient's Reaction:

How did it make you feel?

Week 32

Intentionally invite a co-worker you've never spent time with "off the clock" to dinner or other out of office activity.

BONUS: Do this challenge twice this week.

#IntentionallyGetOverIt

Recipient of your Challenge:

Recipient's Reaction:

How did it make you feel?

Week 33

If you go out to eat, intentionally pick up the tab for another table.

BONUS: Leave a great tip for the wait staff.

#IntentionallyOnYou

Recipient of your Challenge:

Recipient's Reaction:

How did it make you feel?

Week 34

When you arrive at work or your first stop of the day, intentionally walk the parking lot of the building and ensure its litter free.

#IntentionallyKeepingItClean

Recipient of your Challenge:

Recipient's Reaction:

How did it make you feel?

Week 35

Intentionally strike up a conversation with two complete strangers. Learn four things about them and don't forget to log your experience.

BONUS: If you go out to eat, grab coffee, or receive any type of service this week, intentionally ask to speak to the manager and give a compliment about the person who served you.

#IntentionallyMeetNewPeople

Recipient of your Challenge:

Recipient's Reaction:

How did it make you feel?

Week 36

If you go out to eat this week, intentionally leave a 50% tip for your waiter/waitress/bartender

BONUS: Intentionally ask to speak to the manager and give a compliment about the person who served you.

#IntentionallyTip

Recipient of your Challenge:

Recipient's Reaction:

How did it make you feel?

Week 37

At the end of your workday, intentionally write a short message to four of your co-workers or employees letting them know how much you appreciate them. Leave the message at their work center to be surprised their next shift.

BONUS: Let your boss know the things you appreciate about her/him.

#IntentionallyAppreciate

Recipient of your Challenge:

Recipient's Reaction:

How did it make you feel?

<u>Week 38</u>

While at the gas station, intentionally pay for a random individual to pump their gas.

.

BONUS: Ask if they want anything from inside.

#IntentionallyPumpPeopleUp

Recipient of your Challenge:

Recipient's Reaction:

How did it make you feel?

Week 39

Intentionally strike up a conversation with three complete strangers. Learn four things about them and don't forget to log your experience.

BONUS: If you go out to eat, grab coffee, or receive any type of service this week, intentionally ask to speak to the manager and give a compliment about the person who served you.

#IntentionallyMeetNewPeople

Recipient of your Challenge:

Recipient's Reaction:

How did it make you feel?

Week 40

Intentionally volunteer somewhere in your community this week.

BONUS: Take someone with you.

#IntentionallyVolunteer

Recipient of your Challenge:

Recipient's Reaction:

How did it make you feel?

<u>Week 41</u>

While standing in line or in the drive-thru of a coffee shop, intentionally pay for the individual behind you.

BONUS: Pay for the individual in front of you too.

#IntentionallyDrinkOnMe

Recipient of your Challenge:

Recipient's Reaction:

How did it make you feel?

Week 42

Identify someone from your "Reflection Sunday" list who's sick, not doing well, or has hit hard times. Intentionally spend time with her/him, unexpectedly.

BONUS: Bring a gift or card.

#IntentionallyCare

Recipient of your Challenge:

Recipient's Reaction:

How did it make you feel?

Week 43

Intentionally go through this week without complaining...about traffic, coworkers, workload, etc. If you find yourself complaining, go visit a friend from your "Reflection Sunday" list and see how they're doing. Check for any progress on their situation.

BONUS: Volunteer five hours this week at your local hospital.

#IntentionallyPositive

Recipient of your Challenge:

Recipient's Reaction:

How did it make you feel?

Week 44

Intentionally strike up a conversation with *three* complete strangers. Learn four things about them and don't forget to log your experience.

BONUS: If you go out to eat, grab coffee, or receive any type of service this week, intentionally ask to speak to the manager and give a compliment about the person who served you.

#IntentionallyMeetNewPeople

Recipient of your Challenge:

Recipient's Reaction:

How did it make you feel?

Week 45

Intentionally buy two movie gift cards and give them to a single parent you may know who has one child.

BONUS: Buy tickets for a single parent with more than one child.

#IntentionallySaveASeat

Recipient of your Challenge:

Recipient's Reaction:

How did it make you feel?

Week 46

Use this week to intentionally pack up old items of clothes, toys, etc. and donate them to a family who could use them or donate them to a thrift store in your community.

BONUS: Use this week to collect new socks, underwear, etc. from your co-workers and friends and donate them to a local homeless shelter.

#IntentionallyDonate

Recipient of your Challenge:

Recipient's Reaction:

How did it make you feel?

Week 47

Intentionally host a 45-minute "Building Custodian" party for your unsuspecting building custodian. A little cake and ice cream can go a long way.

BONUS: Ask a few of your co-workers to write messages of appreciation to the building custodians and place them in a giftwrapped box for them to open later.

#IntentionallyGrateful

Recipient of your Challenge:

Recipient's Reaction:

How did it make you feel?

Week 48

Intentionally strike up a conversation with three complete strangers. Learn four things about them and don't forget to log your experience.

BONUS: If you go out to eat, grab coffee, or receive any type of service this week, intentionally ask to speak to the manager and give a compliment about the person who served you.

#IntentionallyMeetNewPeople

Recipient of your Challenge:

Recipient's Reaction:

How did it make you feel?

Week 49

When you make dinner, intentionally make a little extra to take to a homeless individual.

BONUS: Make a lot more to feed a few more.

#IntentionallyShare

Recipient of your Challenge:

Recipient's Reaction:

How did it make you feel?

<u>Week 50</u>

While out to lunch, intentionally purchase a gift card from that restaurant and give it to the first person you encounter walking alone.

BONUS: Randomly ask someone sitting alone if you can join them.

#IntentionallyLunchOnMe

Recipient of your Challenge:

Recipient's Reaction:

How did it make you feel?

Week 51

While getting ready for Christmas, intentionally buy a gift for your least favorite person and sincerely give it to her/him.

BONUS: Invite that person to dinner and get to know her/him.

#IntentionallyChangeLives

Recipient of your Challenge:

Recipient's Reaction:

How did it make you feel?

Week 52

CONGRATULATIONS!!!

You made it through your challenge! Use this week to read through your logs. Your intentional acts of kindness have impacted the lives you intentionally set out to change. Please share your story on your social media. Use the hashtag, "#LiveIntentionally," and we'll find it.

Consider buying a few copies of *#LiveIntentionally: 52-Week Challenge* and pass your challenge on to others. Use the next page to log your FULL experience.

#LiveIntentionally

Join our *closed* Facebook community to tell us about your experience:
www.facebook.com/groups/LiveIntentionally

Twitter: @MrBeIntentional
Periscope: @MrBeIntentional
Facebook : www.facebook.com/MrBeIntentional

116

Recipient of your Challenge:

Recipient's Reaction:

How did it make you feel?

About the Author

At the young age of 19, Mark Bush began his law enforcement career as a Correctional Officer with the Dallas County Sheriff's Department in Dallas, TX. He quickly advanced to the position of Detention Training Officer before his 20th birthday. Shortly after Mark's 21st birthday, he made one of the best decisions of his life: he joined the United States Air Force.

While in the Air Force, Mark was able to continue his law enforcement career as a Security Force (Military Police) member. Within three months of getting to his first duty station, Mark deployed to Iraq, December 2004. Two years into his military career, Mark decided to work towards becoming a Military Working Dog Handler. After his hard work and dedication, Mark was selected to join the elite Military Working Dog Program. As a Military Working Dog Handler, Mark deployed to Iraq in 2008 and 2009-2010 as an Explosive Detection Dog Handler. January 5, 2010, Mark and his Military Working Dog "Chukky", were credited with finding a Vehicle Borne Improvised Explosive Device (Car Bomb) with 50 lbs of homemade explosives also saving hundreds of lives. For his meritorious service while deployed to Iraq, The Secretary of the Army awarded Mark with the Army Commendation Medal.

As a handler, Mark was selected to support multiple United States Secret Service missions for; The President and Vice President of the United States, President of Russia, Chief of Staff of the Air Force, Director of the CIA, and Governor Arnold Schwarzenegger. Mark also spent a year of his career as an Air Force Investigator and Joint Drug Task Force Investigator Liaison to the Air Force Office of Special Investigations. Over the span of his eleven year career, Mark received multiple awards. Mark is most proud of his two Air Force Commendation Medals, an Army Commendation Medal, and his Veteran of the Month award from the Mayor of Rapid City, South Dakota.

Mark is currently the Director of Operations for Primecare Home Care Services, Inc. He oversees the day to day operations of four offices that provide expert in-home care solutions (RNs, LPNs, CNAs and PCAs) for seniors and individuals with developmental disabilities.

Mark is also the CEO/President of Saving Grace Security Solutions, LLC. While assigned to the United States Air Force Academy in Colorado Springs, CO from 2004 to 2007, Mark attended New Life Church in Colorado Springs. Mark was actively involved in small groups and the church choir. Shortly after Mark was transferred to Nevada in 2007, his Colorado church family experienced the devastating nightmare of an active shooter. Two members were killed and three were injured after a gunman opened fire as Sunday services were wrapping up.

Mark and his SGSS team tailored training specifically for church leaders based on their military and specialized training to mitigate the most loss of lives possible. Mark is determined to enhance the security mindset of church leaders and their staff to protect their flock.

Mark lives to inspire and impact the lives of the people around him. It's what gives him purpose in his own life.

61059187R00078

Made in the USA
Charleston, SC
09 September 2016